INVESTING IN
GOLD and SILVER
BULLION

THE ULTIMATE SAFE HAVEN INVESTMENTS

ALEX UWAJEH

Legal Disclaimers

This book is presented to you for informational purposes only and is not a substitution for any professional advice. The contents herein are based on the views and opinions of the author and all associated contributors.

While every effort has been made by the author and all associated contributors to present accurate and up to date information within this document, it is apparent technologies rapidly change. Therefore, the author and all associated contributors reserve the right to update the contents and information provided herein as these changes progress. The author and/or all associated contributors take no responsibility for any errors or omissions if such discrepancies exist within this document.

The author and all other contributors accept no responsibility for any consequential actions taken, whether monetary, legal, or otherwise, by any and all readers of the materials provided.

It is the readers sole responsibility to seek professional advice before taking any action on their part.

Readers results will vary based on their skill level and individual perception of the contents herein, and thus no guarantees, monetarily or otherwise, can be made accurately. Therefore, no guarantees are made.

Acknowledgements

Big thanks to David McDonald who pointed
me in the direction of Gold and Silver Bullion.
Thanks also to the WBC bullion club
members.

As always, I give God all the glory for the completion of this book.

Table of Contents

Introduction: Why Gold and Silver?

There are two large categories of metals: precious metals and base metals. This categorization is based on the metal's ability to resist oxidation and corrosion. Precious metals have a higher resistance to corrosion while base metals have a much lower tolerance.

In this book, we will be looking at two precious metals: gold and silver. We will look at the fundamentals of these precious metals and show you *why* and *when* it's a good idea for your investment portfolio to have some exposure to these precious metals. From what drives their price, including how they can be used as a gauge of investor sentiment regarding the stability and future of the economy, to investment vehicles, this guide will help you gain a better understanding of gold and silver.

All that Glitters May Not Be Gold…

…but its value cannot be denied. For thousands of years, gold has been used as a form of currency and has not lost its inherent value. Its metallurgical properties have made it a highly valued asset throughout the centuries, including its virtual indestructibility and rarity.

The Properties of Gold

Gold is one of the few metals to have an incredibly high level of resistance to corrosion. Exposure to oxygen, for example, has practically no effect on this metal, allowing it to retain its properties for thousands of years with no change.

In terms of rarity, you are likely well aware that this is one of the rarest resources on the planet and in over 6,000 years, ever since gold was first mined, only about 150,000 tons of gold have been extracted in total. This is a tiny amount, especially when compared to other metals.

Another advantage gold has is that it is a very malleable metal, making it easy to shape into almost anything.

This has made gold one of the favourite metals for jewellery makers all over the world. However, it is often mixed in alloys with other metals to allow it to retain its shape because in pure form (24K), it can be too soft to wear.

Ductility is a measurement that refers to how much wire a certain amount of metal can produce. For example, one ounce of gold can be converted into more than 50 miles of wire that can be used in a variety of electronic applications, making it incredibly valuable in this industry.

The Value of Gold to Investors

Gold's properties have allowed it to maintain its value for thousands of years, which makes it a great investment vehicle. However, you will find there are two schools of thought when it comes to gold and other precious metals. There are those who believe gold is a great hedge against currency devaluation and feel investing in gold is a wise course of action at any time, especially for capital preservation.

Then, on the opposite end of the spectrum are those who believe gold is a waste of time and money because it no longer has any value in the digital age and will soon be worthless to everyone.

While there will always be naysayers, no one can deny the fact that gold's value has remained unchanged since recorded history, which is why it was even used as currency for a lot longer than we have had paper money and fiat currencies. In fact, even when we switched to paper money, gold was still used to back the currency and it was only in 1971 that the gold standard was eliminated by President Nixon. Many feel this decision was what led to the continued devaluation of the dollar.

But wait, the price of gold fluctuates thousands of times daily. How can anyone say its value has remained the same? It's a good question and the answer is quite simple. We all try to determine the value of something based on price, i.e. its dollar value. However, the dollar, or any currency, is just a piece of paper so a true measurement of value would be how much oil you can buy with an ounce of gold. Or, how much food you can buy, for example.

24 Hour Gold Price Chart spanning 5 days
courtesy of www.GoldSilver.com

Two or three centuries ago, you could buy a
high quality suit or clothes with an ounce of
gold and the same holds true today. So, gold

hasn't actually changed its value.
It's the currency that has appreciated or depreciated over time, which is one of the factors driving the price of gold. We'll take a closer look at precious metal prices a little later.

Besides the stability of gold's value, there are other considerations that make it an attractive investment, including some of the industries it is used in. There is a high demand for gold in the jewellery sector, as you probably imagined, but it is also a highly coveted metal in the electronics industry, as well as in dentistry. The more industries use a metal, the higher the demand for that metal will be, which will often drive prices up even further.

Is It Time to Melt the Silverware?

Jewellery and silverware represent a small percentage of the silver market, as this metal has wide range of practical applications, from technology to healthcare and photography. In fact, over 65 percent of total silver consumption can be attributed to the industrial sector. Due to the fact that it has a high resistance to corrosion and oxidation and because of its numerous practical applications, silver has always been considered an attractive investment.

Silver Applications and Demand

Silver is used in a wide range of sectors, from fashion to décor, technology and industry. However, you might not realize exactly how widespread the use of silver is. For example, in recent years, the technology sector has expanded its use of silver massively.

It is one of the best thermal and electrical conductors in the world, which, in combination with other properties it has, makes it the only suitable option for certain applications. Not only is it used in electrical components but it is also used as a coating material for data storage media, such as DVDs. Essentially, almost all the electronic devices we use today have some degree of silver in them.

Additionally, it is also used in the photography sector, in water purification, and even in windows and glass. There are so many applications for this precious metal that demand has soared over the past ten years and currently the supply of silver cannot meet the demand.

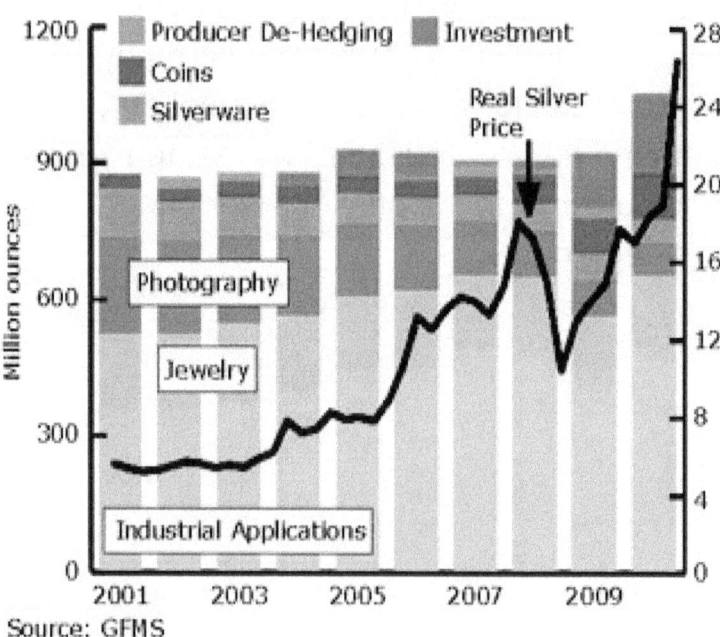

World Silver Demand

Source: GFMS

This increase in demand is one of the factors that has influenced the price of silver, driving it

up significantly, as you can see in the
previous chart.

The Value of Silver to Investors

Similar to gold, silver has long been
considered a safe investment, especially to
hedge against inflation. Like gold, silver is a
precious metal and has been used historically
as a currency. While not quite as rare as gold
or some other precious metals, it is still
relatively rare and its unique properties have
allowed it to maintain its value over many
thousands of years.

It is considered to be a low-risk and cost-
effective investment, especially since it is
relatively protected from the volatility of the
financial markets. It is worth noting, though,
that the cost or perceived value of silver is
much more volatile than gold. Despite this, it
is still considered an effective hedge against
currency devaluation and an excellent vehicle
for capital preservation.

Many investors opt for silver because it offers a level of stability due to its intrinsic value. Including silver in their investment portfolios is also another step they can take to diversify their assets, thus protecting their wealth against market volatility.

Currencies, the Gold Standard and Precious Metals

The gold standard was in use in the US until 1971. This meant the value of the US dollar was pegged to the value of gold. However, as European and Asian countries began buying up US gold reserves, President Nixon decided to eliminate the gold standard and the dollar, as well as any other currency that followed suit, has been declining in value ever since.

The devaluation occurred mainly because governments had no other option than to create additional currency to combat short-term economic crisis, as the recent financial meltdown is testament to.

Other economic policies were adopted that further damaged the value of currency, including extending cheap credit, which resulted in spending by both organizations and individuals that could not be supported for the long-term, tax breaks, interest rate changes to support cheap lending, and foreign borrowing, which increased the deficit.

However, an interesting process began to occur: as the value of the dollar against gold dropped.

The value of precious metals began to rise. This is because investors began to see these commodities as the only safe haven in an economy where the value of currency had begun to plummet. As the chart below shows, gold was selling for approximately $40 per ounce in 1971, a price it had been hovering around for more than two decades, only to double in less than two years. A decade later it was selling for a massive $615 per ounce, an increase of 1,500%

Evolution of the Price of Gold

1970 - 2011

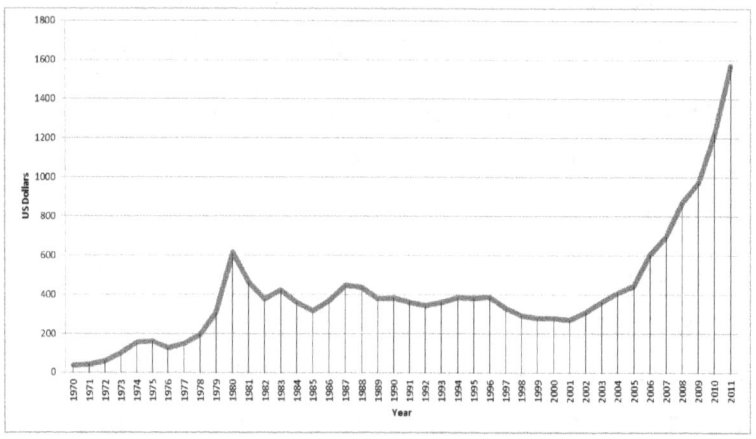

So, how does the elimination of the gold standard affect the current market?

Due to the financial meltdown of 2008 and the fact that many economies have not yet recovered, with many countries still hovering on the verge of recession, countries are continuing to create more currency to try and prop up their economies. Of course, the term used nowadays is quite elevated: quantitative easing.

Quantitative easing simply means the central banks have decided to pump new currency into the market, in the hopes of stimulating the economy. However, while more cash might stimulate spending, it simply means injecting more paper money into circulation. This leads to further devaluation of the currency in question, which is why we are seeing price increases across the board.

As the dollar loses value, many investors are turning to precious metals, converting at least part of their investment portfolio from cash, equities and other assets into silver and gold in an attempt to preserve the value of their capital. This is why the price of gold has more than doubled since 2007, when it was selling for approximately $695 per ounce. In 2011, the average price of one ounce of gold was $1,571.

Three Reasons to Invest in Precious Metals

So, why should you invest in precious metals, especially gold and silver?

Capital Preservation

Capital preservation is probably the most common objective of investors when they invest in precious metals. Essentially, they are hedging against currency devaluation. It is a way for them to protect their wealth.

Think of it as the equivalent of purchasing insurance on your home. If your house catches fire, you will receive the full value of your property from your insurance policy. The same applies to purchasing gold and silver.

As we've already discussed, even if the currency drops in value, gold and silver will maintain their value, which makes them an ideal investment vehicle for anyone looking to preserve their capital.

However, remember that if you are purchasing gold and silver with capital preservation in mind that means you are basically expecting the dollar to drop in value.

Capital Appreciation

Just because precious metals are a safe haven and often used as a hedge, it doesn't mean they can't be used for capital appreciation as well.

Through speculation, you can buy and sell precious metals and make a profit, especially in an economy such as this one, where the prices of gold and silver have been rising steadily over the past few years.

However, you have to remember that the only way you will really make a profit is if the devaluation of the dollar is slower. Otherwise, you will be simply preserving your capital and in this situation it's probably smarter to hang on to your gold and silver.

Cash Flow

Another reason to invest in gold and silver is for cash flow purposes. In other words, you're aiming to create an additional income stream. Basically, it's like purchasing a property that you intend to rent out. It will bring you an annual income for as long as you own it, irrespective of its value.

There are many benefits to this approach. First of all, you will be hedging your wealth by owning gold and silver, but you will also be making profit every year.

Essentially, it doesn't really matter how the value of these precious metals fluctuates because you will still be making money every year, so you can afford to hang on to these assets for the long term and won't have to worry about the volatility of the markets.

There are a few ways you can use gold and silver to generate cash flow. The first is through short-term speculation, i.e. commodity trading. Essentially, you purchase gold or silver and sell it within a relatively short timeframe for a profit. This could be anywhere from a few minutes to a few months, depending on your trading strategy.

Another method is to invest in these precious metals via dividend stocks in mining companies. The advantage to this approach is that you can grow your wealth by reinvesting your dividends into more equity. However, remember that via this approach you won't actually be holding physical gold and there are other factors affecting the price of shares, including the company's fundamentals, which are often unrelated to the price of gold. We'll look at more investment vehicles for precious metals later on.

The State of the Economy and Precious Metals

The state of the economy can often be used as a gauge for the price of precious metals. The worse the economy is performing, the more the price of precious metals will rise. One way to determine where the economy will be heading is to look at the GDP and deficit.

The GDP or Gross Domestic Product is basically everything a country produces and sells, which is what brings money to the state via taxes. If the GDP is low relative to the deficit, then the only solution for most governments is to print more currency. This leads to further currency devaluation.

For example, the US is predicted to be approximately $16.5 trillion in deficit by November, 2012. However, that's not the only problem. The baby boomers are soon going to hit retirement age and the social security and healthcare systems will have to deliver, meaning the government has massive off-balance-sheet promises to keep to these people alone. So, it could be a while before the situation improves.

Another gauge of the economy, and a way to really determine how dire the situation is, is by looking at the price of credit-default swaps. When a country has a high level of debt and a low GDP, sentiment regarding its ability to pay off its debt on time is far from positive. So, to ensure that debt credit default swaps are purchased, CDS indexes are used by traders to determine the credit quality of a country or company. This is because the more the price rises, the worse the situation is.

Therefore, if you see the price of credit default swaps soaring, then the market might be telling you it's a perfect opportunity to purchase precious metals.

Currently, for example, the price of European CDSs is at an all-time high, meaning the situation isn't looking good and printing even more currency seems to be the only solution. This will lead to further devaluation and investors will turn to precious metals as a hedge, driving the price up even further.

And the future certainly doesn't look bright, with Europe hovering on the verge of recession, even with the austerity measures that have been instituted. There is even talk of some countries leaving the Eurozone and returning to their original currencies. This will only lead to massive inflation within those countries as they print more and more of their own currencies to try and cover the deficit.

Even the US doesn't look quite as rosy as some believe, with the deficit continually on the rise. In fact, it's very likely spending will continue to increase, which will probably lead to further need for quantitative easing and it is likely we will see the value of the dollar fall even further as a result.

What Influences the Price of Gold and Silver?

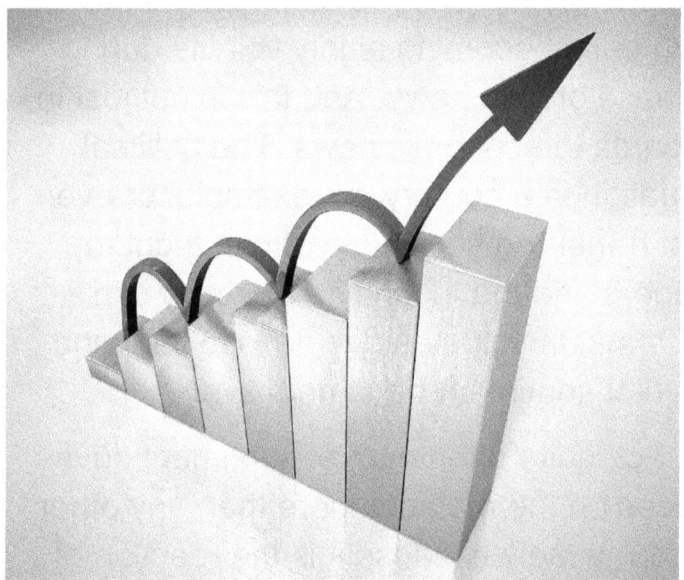

There are many factors that influence the price of precious metals but these are some of the most important ones.

Market Sentiment

All markets are driven by trader and investment sentiment to a certain degree.

If you've ever traded, you will know how various pieces of news affect the markets, with price becoming highly volatile during release of said news. And this is not just in regards to economic news. The political situation in a country, for example, or even just rumoured social unrest can frighten traders and that country's currency can plummet in value as people lose faith and market sentiment turns negative.

In fact, quite often market sentiment drives prices on the markets more than any other factor, simply because it is the reaction of traders to economic news and reports that leads to the buying and selling of assets, which drives supply and demand on the markets.

For example, in terms of equities, even if a company posts good results, its stock prices can fall if a rumour is started. If a rumour is started claiming the company is considering cutting dividends, let's say, to increase the proportion of the profits it is allocating to growth and reinvestment. It could be a simple rumour and hold no truth at all, but if the source is 'credible' then value investors will rush to offload their stocks before the price drops too far. Gold and silver react in much the same way. In the late 1990s and all the way up to 2007, investors avoided gold like the plague. It was a time of massive economic growth and everyone was looking towards asset classes that would bring massive profits. No one wanted to hear about gold because it doesn't offer interest, nor is it traditionally a profitable investment. It was, and still is, mainly used for capital preservation, and at a time of massive growth in other asset classes, no one was interested in capital preservation. Everyone was running after capital gains, especially since the market was offering massive returns.

Let's not forget all the derivatives that appeared on the market as financial institutions found new and better ways to make money by inventing more and more complex financial instruments most investors had a hard time understanding. However, market sentiment was along the lines of "why understand it when I can make a fortune off it?"

When traders were posting massive returns from trading everything from equities to currency, who wanted gold? There was no need for capital preservation. The economy was booming and there was no end in sight. That was until 2008, when the bubble burst in a highly spectacular way.

Suddenly, gold was the safe haven every investor was clamoring to buy, especially after they had been burned so badly when the stock market took a plunge that forced some from riches to rags.

As a result, the price of gold climbed from approximately $695 in 2007 to over $1,600, which it is trading at now, at the beginning of 2012.

Currency

The value of gold is quoted in US dollars but it is mainly purchased by individuals using other currencies, which means the price of gold will go up as the dollar drops. There are two ways to look at it. First, if viewed as a commodity, the falling dollar would mean negative investor sentiment, leading to increased buying of gold.

On the other hand, if gold is considered a currency, then when the dollar falls, gold has to rise by definition and the reverse is also true.

It is important to note that while there is some correlation between the dollar and the price of gold, the gold market doesn't move in the same way as other precious metal markets.

For example, when it comes to silver, the main driver is supply and demand. The higher the demand and the lower the supply, the higher the price will climb. However, when it comes to gold, things are a little different.

The price of gold tends to show more restrained movement in response to decreased supply and production. One reason is because there are large stockpiles of gold, which can't be said for silver. Thus, if central banks feel the price of gold is too high, they can release some of their reserves to drive the price down. So, essentially, the market tends to place less weight on news related to supply and demand when making its trading decisions.

The currency component is one of the main factors affecting the price of gold in the long term, and even silver to a certain degree. As currency devalues, more and more investors turn to precious metals as a hedge, driving up the price of these precious metals.

Interest Rates

An environment of low interest rates is positive for almost any asset class, including precious metals. However, for precious metals, high interest rates made them a commodity everyone wanted to avoid. Why invest in an asset that couldn't possibly deliver.

Well, this situation lasted for a while, until it was decided the economy needed further stimulation and interest rates began to drop, allowing cheap credit to be extended to the population.

The results of that decision, as well as highly lenient banking regulations and other policies, are rather obvious.

Mining

Another factor influencing the price of precious metals, especially gold, is mining.

The fact is that production has decreased significantly over the past few years, because there is little gold available in 'easy-to-access' conditions.

Essentially, all the 'low-hanging fruit' has been mined and any new discoveries are usually in areas that are very difficult to mine. You can see how production cost are rising when you consider the fact that it can take a decade to get all the permits required to mine this precious metals. One shouldn't forget that there are other factors influencing production costs, including the rising prices of other resources required to mine gold.

Portfolio Diversification and Precious Metals

After the recent financial crisis, an ever increasing number of financial institutions, including private banks, pension funds and hedge funds have turned to the commodity markets to diversify their portfolios.

The more currency is printed, the more gold and silver they purchase because they know gold will always maintain its intrinsic value and many of these organizations are currently looking more to preserve their capital than necessarily making profit.

This is mainly due to the fact that physical gold is highly liquid, making it easy to sell in any market conditions. Even in the worst case scenario, where currencies become worthless, physical gold can still be traded for goods because of its intrinsic value.

And these large market movers are not the only ones turning to gold and silver as a hedge. More and more retail investors are allocating part of their portfolio to gold and silver in an effort to preserve their capital.

How to Get Exposure to Gold and Silver

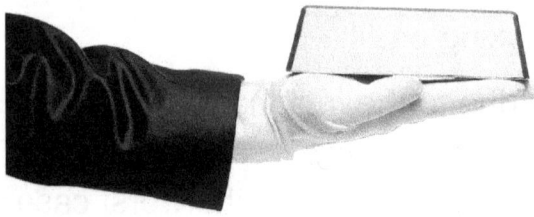

There are a wide range of methods for the individual investor to gain exposure to precious metals. Whether you are interested in physically owning gold and silver in the form of coins or bullion, or prefer to go for less traditional options such as mining stocks and other more complex financial instruments related to precious metals, the best precious metal investments will largely depend on how you view the future and what your personal goals are.

Even if you do want to invest in physical gold or silver, don't worry because there are plenty of options available to you without you having to take physical delivery.

Physical Gold: Bars and Coins

The first gold coins were struck by King Croesus during his reign in western Asia Minor. Ever since then, gold coins have been considered a form of legal tender.

The advantage for the retail investor when it comes to coins and small bars is that you don't have to buy massive quantities to be able to include gold in your investment portfolio. The fact that gold purchased for investment purposes is exempt from Value Added Tax in many countries is an added bonus.

Gold Bullion Coins

There are plenty of options when it comes to gold bullion coins because many governments across the world issue this form of tender. In the countries they are issued, the value is not based on the content of gold but rather their face value.

Conversely, when it comes to global market value, it is calculated based on the fine gold content with a premium added, which differs depending on the coin and dealer.

The smaller the coin, the higher the premium will be as it covers production costs as well as the dealer's commission.

Coins come in a variety of sizes, starting from as small as 1/20th of an ounce all the way up to 1,000 grams. However, the most widespread sizes are 1/20, 1/10, 1/4, 1/2 and one troy ounce of fine gold content. Remember that bullion coins have nothing to do with commemorative or numismatic coins. These are valued according to the quality of their design and finish as well as their rarity and not their fine gold content like bullion coins.

Below are some examples of gold bullion coins minted by different countries.

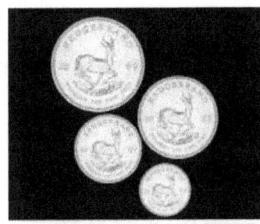

South African Krugerrand

Australian Kangaroo

American

American

Britannia

Images courtesy of Gold Bars Worldwide

Gold Bars

There are two types of gold bars, depending on how they are manufactured. Thus, there are cast and minted bars. Gold bars themselves are considered to be any gold item, irrespective of its shape, that was produced by a recognized bar manufacturer. They are usually sold at a price that consists of the value of the fine gold content plus a low premium.

Usually, the markings featured on the bars tend to reveal the name of the manufacturer, the weight of the bar and the level of gold purity. Some bars also feature a serial number. The characteristics of bars tend to change according to the manufacturer and the area they are produced. Furthermore, gold bars are categorized by weight.

Thus, small gold bars are considered to be equal or below 1,000 g (approximately 32 oz), while large bars are those weighing more than one kilogram.

Small bars are generally preferred by investors due to the lower entry barrier and smaller investment of capital required at one time. There are more than 50 different weights of small bars manufactured worldwide, providing investors with a wide range of options. Gold purity generally is around 99.5% but it can vary slightly between manufacturers. If you wish to further investigate accredited bar manufacturers and the international gold bar market, please visit the Gold Bars Worldwide website at www.goldbarsworldwide.com.

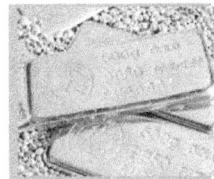

Gold Futures and Options

Another option for investors looking to get exposure to gold is via gold futures and options.

Gold Futures

Like any other futures contract, gold futures represent a binding commitment to deliver or accept delivery of a certain quantity of gold at certain level of purity on a pre-determined date at a pre-agreed price. Investors pay a cash deposit to the broker, referred to as the initial margin, and represents only a small percentage of the underlying asset.

The advantage to gold futures is that you can make significant trading profits because you can buy a lot more gold than if you were to purchase it in physical form. However, it should be remembered that they can also lead to significant losses. Futures contracts are traded on regulated commodity exchanges, with the largest being the New York Mercantile Exchange Comex Division, now known as CME Globex, the Chicago Board of Trade and the Tokyo Commodity Exchange. These futures also trade on the India and Dubai commodity exchanges.

Gold Options

Gold options give their owner the right to buy (call options) or sell (put options) a certain amount of gold at a pre-agreed price and on a set date. Note that it is merely the right and the owner is not obligated in any way to fulfill the contract.

The price of options depends on a wide range of factors, including interest rates, volatility, time until they expire, the spot price of gold and the pre-agreed price.

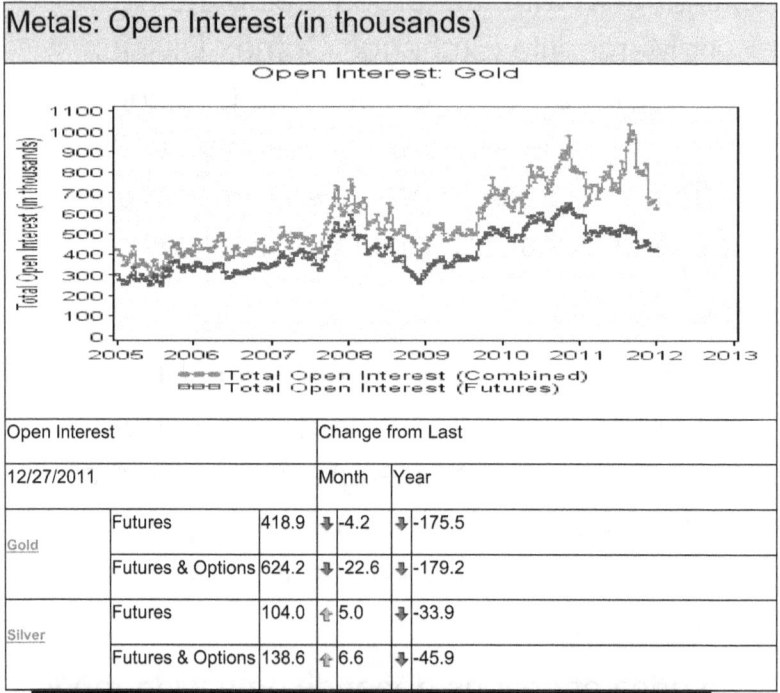

Metals: Open Interest (in thousands)

Open Interest: Gold

Open Interest			Change from Last	
12/27/2011			Month	Year
Gold	Futures	418.9	⬇ -4.2	⬇ -175.5
	Futures & Options	624.2	⬇ -22.6	⬇ -179.2
Silver	Futures	104.0	⬆ 5.0	⬇ -33.9
	Futures & Options	138.6	⬆ 6.6	⬇ -45.9

Chart courtesy of the Commodity Futures Trading Commission

Gold Exchange Traded Funds

Exchange Traded Funds (ETFs) backed by gold are traded on many stock exchanges all over the world.

These are financial instruments that are regulated and meant to offer investors the opportunity to gain exposure to gold price.

ETFs are a great way for investors to integrate gold into their investment portfolios because they are cost effective and highly secure. Additionally, it is also more efficient because you don't have to take actual delivery of the gold. ETFs are responsible for the increase in attractiveness of gold as a way to diversify one's investment portfolio.

Gold Warrants

Similar to futures and options but mainly used by leading investment banks, gold warrants give the holder the right to purchase gold at a specified price at a particular future date. As with futures and options, the buyer pays a premium for this right, allowing them to lock in a certain price and make a profit if the market moves in the forecasted direction.

Gold Accounts

Bullion banks, which are those banks that deal in precious metals, offer investors two types of gold accounts. Thus, there are allocated accounts and unallocated accounts.

Allocated Gold Accounts

The allocated gold account is similar to keeping your gold in a safe and is considered to be the safest way to invest in physical gold because the gold is held in a special vault that a dealer or repository owns and manages. Bars or coins are created and stamped with a number and hallmark. They are then allocated to the individual investors who also pay a premium for insurance and storage, besides the standard price of the bullion they are purchasing.

Note that if you choose this route, you own the gold and are simply using the dealer's services so you don't need to worry about issues such as storage. This means the holder of the gold, i.e. the dealer, may not lend, sell, borrow, lease or do anything with those gold bars unless it is at your specific instructions.

Unallocated Gold Accounts

There is one problem, namely that bullion banks tend to deal only in large quantities so if you are intending to open an account with less than 1,000 ounces, you might have to look at other options. This is because they generally work with institutional customers such as private banks, central banks and large participants in the gold market.

Gold Pool Accounts

These are a good option for the smaller investor who wants to open an account with less than 1,000 ounces. Basically, you are buying a share in a Gold Pool Account and can purchase as little as one ounce.

Electronic Currencies

Another option is the electronic currency. There are some electronic currencies available that are backed by gold bullion which is in an allocated account. This is a simple and inexpensive way to buy and sell gold, with the advantage of being able to use it as money as well. You can purchase any quantity of gold you like and you can use it to make payments online all over the world.

Gold Accumulation Plans

Gold Accumulation Plans or GAPs are like a traditional savings plan except instead of setting cash aside every month, you convert it into gold. So, say you get paid on the 30th of every month and you want to allocate $500 every month to your GAP. That money would then be deducted from your paycheck and used to purchase gold on the first trading day after the cash hits the account.

The advantage is that you can allocate small amounts of cash every month and you won't have to pay the premium coins and bars usually come with.

Additionally, since you are buying small amounts of gold regularly, over a long period of time, you will not be as exposed to short-term volatility in gold price.

The contract is usually for a minimum of one year but afterwards you can terminate it and either pick up your gold in the form of coins or bars. You also have the option to sell the gold and get cash instead.

Gold Mining Stocks

A popular option, especially for investors looking for capital gains, is purchasing equity in gold mining companies. This offers the unique opportunity to gain exposure to gold while also being able to make a profit and even improve cash flow via dividend stocks.

While this is an excellent investment option it shouldn't be considered an alternative to investing in physical gold. Stocks are driven by the price of gold but there are also other factors involved including the fundamentals of the mines, the reserves of unmined gold, projects and so on. Of course, it is these factors that offer investors the opportunity for capital appreciation.

However, as with any investment in equity, one needs to make sure to do their due diligence, which includes getting to know the mining industry, studying the financials of the company being considered and conducting technical analysis on both the price of gold as well as the stocks in question.

Gold Certificates

Gold certificates are simply ownership papers of physical gold, proving you own it even though it is being stored by the bank that issued the certificate. The advantages include the fact that you don't have to worry about insurance costs and storage as well as safety. Likewise, it's much easier to sell your gold this way because it can be done either online or via a phone call to the bank. Not all countries issue these gold certificates but they are more prevalent in Germany and Switzerland. The Perth Mint also issues such certificates and they are backed by the government of Western Australia. It might be an option for you as they are distributed to quite a few other countries.

Gold Oriented Funds

These funds include a number of vehicles focused on collective investments, including mutual funds and unit trusts.

Some of these funds specialize in gold and equity in gold mining companies. You have to analyze each fund individually because they have different structures and objectives. Some will invest in shares looking for capital gains specifically in gold mining companies while others prefer value investments and look for companies that mine other minerals as well. Other differences include the types of assets the fund will invest in, with some preferring a more diverse approach, investing in futures as well as equity, while others might prefer a mix of physical gold and futures.

The type of fund you invest in is wholly determined by your goals and how you want your investment portfolio to be allocated. Remember, though, it is always a good idea to have some form of ownership of physical gold, especially if you are looking to hedge against currency devaluation.

The risk of investing in gold funds is the same as the risk of investing directly in the different financial instruments. The advantage, though, is that you can get exposure to a wider range of instruments than you could if you were to invest directly due to the collective nature of these funds.

Gold Structured Products

While structured products have a high entry barrier since they are designed mainly for large financial institutions, it is still worth taking a look at these products for a complete understanding of the gold market.

Forwards

Forwards are similar to futures except that they trade over the counter and usually the two parties involved will negotiate the price and date directly. Unlike futures, which are guaranteed by the exchange, forwards carry the risk of one of the parties not fulfilling the agreement. Another disadvantage to forward contracts is that the obligation cannot be transferred meaning the holding institution cannot sell it to another party before the contract matures.

Gold Backed Bonds and Structured Notes

Investors use gold backed bonds as a way to gain exposure to the fluctuations of gold price, to obtain a yield and for capital preservation.

These bonds are issued by large investment banks and bullion dealers.

A structured note takes part of amount being invested and puts it into options while the rest goes towards more traditional products to try and generate capital gains.

Silver Investment Vehicles

Silver investment vehicles are, in most cases, exactly the same as gold. Thus, you can invest in silver via:

- Silver bars with a purity of 99.9%;
- Silver coins minted by governments;
- Medallions: pieces of round silver that look like coins but are not considered to be legal tender;
- Certificates or Storage Accounts;
- Accumulation plans;
- Futures contracts;
- Options;
- Exchange Traded Funds;
- Equity in mining specialized mining companies;
- Mutual Funds

Each of these comes with its own set of advantages and disadvantages. For example, if you opt for physical silver, such as bars, coins or medallions, you have a wide range of options because they tend to be the least expensive option and can be converted into cash anywhere in the world.

It is worth noting that no matter which investment vehicle you choose, the price of silver is much more volatile than gold. For example, at the beginning of 2011 it was trading at around $25 - $30, only to rise to almost $50 and fall back down towards the end of the year to around $29.

Thus, it is wise to take a more cautious approach when investing in silver. However, this volatility lends itself relatively well to making short-term profits, but as with any form of trading, there is also great risk of loss involved.

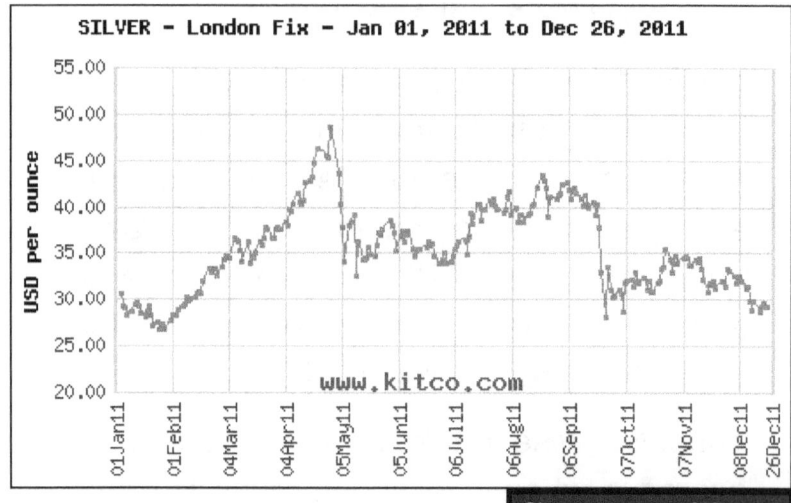

Chart courtesy of Kitco at
www.kitco.com

Investing in Precious Metals

Now that we've looked at why you should invest in precious metals and what vehicles are available for you to do this, let's look at

What you should be looking for when investing in precious metals.

Understand What You Are Investing In

First of all, no matter what type of investment vehicle you are opting for, you need to know the industry and sovereign fundamentals.

Industry fundamentals means that you have to analyze the gold and silver industry, including supply and demand, market sentiment and so on and so forth. However, as we revealed earlier, the state of the global economy can have a significant impact on the price of precious metals, which is why you should be looking at sovereign fundamentals as well.

Sovereign fundamentals have more to do with precious metals and currency. Basically, you are analyzing the financial statements of the major economies in the world, as we explained previously. The higher the chances of further quantitative easing being required, for example, the better the chance of the price of gold and silver going up as investors turn to these precious metals as a hedge.

The idea is that the better your understanding of the movements in price of gold and silver, the easier it will be for you to make the right call, especially since all investment vehicles for these precious metals are driven, at least in part, by the price of the underlying asset.

Besides fundamentals, you also need to look at the technical data of the gold, silver and currencies. This is because fundamental data will signal the existence or lack of an opportunity but technical data provides you with the timing. Technical analysis will allow you to pick the right moment to enter the market to ensure you get the maximum benefit from your investment. This applies no matter what your objective is because even if you simply want to purchase gold, for example, as a hedge, if the price is too high, you won't be able to hedge anything. So, timing is critical.

Make a Plan

You need to build an investment plan, no matter what type of investment you are making. However, with the numerous options available when it comes to precious metals, this is even more important. You need to decide what types of investment vehicles you will be using to gain exposure to precious metals and these depend mainly on your objectives.

For example, if your main goal is to purchase gold and silver as a hedge, then you will probably want to look towards purchasing the physical metal, either directly and taking delivery or via an ETF or Gold Pool Account.

If your objective is capital appreciation, then you might consider purchasing equity in gold mining companies.

If you want to improve your cash flow, then you might opt to trade these metals on the markets, or look towards futures and options.

Then again, you can decide you want to do all three and use a mix of these vehicles, allocating various percentages of your available capital to each objective. The more risk averse you are, the more you should lean towards lower risk options, namely physical gold and silver, with a smaller portion of your investment portfolio being allocated to equity and other vehicles that provide capital gains.

Remember, any form of trading, namely buying and selling any of the investment vehicles we mentioned for short-term profit, carries substantial risk of losses so make sure to never invest money you cannot afford to lose.

Some questions the World Gold Council recommends you should answer before taking the leap include:

Why have you decided to purchase precious metals? What's your objective?

Do you want an asset that you can physically touch or gain access to at all times or do you simply want to take advantage of the price fluctuations of precious metals?

Do you want the precious metal delivered to your door or would you prefer the security of a vault?

Do you know exactly how much the transaction will cost, including all the taxes, commissions, premiums, storage and insurance?

Is the seller (either a dealer, broker or person) who you intend to buy from trustworthy and reliable?

What role will precious metals play in your investment portfolio and how will it fit in with the other investments you have?

These are just a few of the questions you need to answer before investing in precious metals.

Investing in Gold Equities

Investing in equities is quite different to investing in the physical asset itself since there are many more risks involved. However, there is also a better chance of capital appreciation so it's definitely worth taking a look at. We'll be looking mainly at investing in stocks in gold mining companies but the principles also apply to silver mining companies.

When it comes to investing in a gold mining company, the core principles of stock investing are the same. Thus, you should never put more money in the market than you can afford to lose. Just because a gold mining company is selling cheap, don't jump on the opportunity without doing your homework first because it could be a junior company who is only prospecting for gold. Since only one company in over two hundred finds gold, you could be looking at some completely worthless stock.

Therefore, it is critical that you do your homework first and ask who the promoter of the stock is. How effective has he or she been at creating wealth for investors? And you need to find out who the best performers in the industry are. And remember: never invest money you can't afford to lose.

As with the industry, you need to know exactly what you are buying. Dig up all the information you can on the company. Read their annual reports and not just the latest ones but go back a few years to see how the company performed both during good and bad times for the industry.

Remember that an economic boom generally means bad times for the gold industry so make sure to go back a few years and see how the company performed. Not only that, you might want to look at the management of the company as well. All you have to do is call up and ask and you'll be surprised how willing these companies are to give you everything you need.

Often, small company stocks are sold by promoters. These are generally those phone calls or emails you get telling you about this amazing new stock in an up-and-coming super amazing gold company that you'll regret not buying into because stock prices will explode. Yes, you've probably had plenty of those.

However, not all of them are bad, but again, you need to do your due diligence. Investigate the person promoting the stock and see if they've ever had any problems, including fraud charges, tax evasions, bankruptcy proceedings and so on and so forth. You are looking for someone honest and if they've been in the business for a while and haven't had any issues, then they just might be for real. Remember that you can always ask your peers about their success with a particular promoter and that's an excellent way of finding out who is really good at what they do and not just at selling and promoting.

Greed is a killer in any form of financial investment or trading. It's what makes us hang on to those stocks when we know we should get out and take our profits and then we watch in horror as the market reverses and the shares drop in value. So, if you are investing in a junior company or looking for capital appreciation, don't wait an eternity to offload those stocks or you might find yourself on the losing end of the stick. If you want to invest in stocks that can keep you without worrying about volatility, consider dividend stocks as these will bring you a good annual return and the companies tend to be much more stable.

On the opposite end of the spectrum is fear of loss. People are generally terrified of losing even a penny, which can lead to investors keeping stocks that are clearly losers because they are hoping that by some miracle the market will reverse and they will at least break even. This is the best way to lose all your capital. Set a maximum amount you are willing to lose and once you hit that ceiling, get out. You might miss one or two profitable investments when the stocks retrace but that's a lot better than ending up with a pile of stocks that are worthless.

The Fundamentals of Gold Stocks or How to Improve Your Odds

There are so many small gold companies that it can be difficult to sort through them if you don't know exactly what fundamentals you should be looking at. The following fundamentals can be used to analyze any gold company, from the junior ones to the intermediate and senior gold companies.

Management

One factor few investors consider when analyzing a company is the management. You need to learn as much as you can about them and especially how much they know about the industry and what their training is. For example, are they geologists or lawyers? How much experience do they have in the industry? Do they really know what they are doing? The more effective the management team is, the better the chances of the company being successful over the long term, which implies better returns for the investor.

Market Capitalization

Market capitalization refers to the number of outstanding shares multiplied by the value of each individual share.

In other words, if a company has 3 million outstanding shares at $2 a piece, then the company is worth $6 million. The question you need to ask yourself is whether or not that company is worth $6 million.

One way to do that is to find out how many ounces of gold the company has in reserve, i.e. in the ground, and what the market price per ounce is. So, let's say they have half a million ounces in the ground and the market price is $100 per ounce, then the company should be valued at $50 million, which means the company is undervalued.

On the other end of the spectrum, if the company only has cash but no gold reserves, most investment strategists recommend that you shouldn't pay more than double the cash per share.

The key is to buy into companies that are undervalued because it provides a wider buffer of safety.

Money

If you are looking at a gold exploration company, you have to think like an entrepreneur. You need to remember that it takes time for any startup to start producing money and in mining it takes even longer with practically no cash flow coming in. These companies spend exorbitant amounts of money before they can sell their first ounce of gold.

As an investor, you need to determine what the chances of these delays taking place are and whether or not the company will have to find additional financing, usually through the sale of more shares. This is an even bigger problem if the company has been unable to make a find as it will lead to drastic drop in share price.

Minerals

When it comes to gold mining companies, those whose principal production is gold are valued higher than those that produce both gold and copper. However, when gold prices start to soar, these companies are treated exactly the same as those that produce only gold, which makes them a much better option for investors because they are cheaper to buy into.

Life of the Mine

When it comes to mining company stocks, these tend to be volatile, especially in the period before production begins. At first, when a find is made, stocks soar because every one is ecstatic thinking they are going to make a killing. However, when people realize it will take a while to actually get the gold out of the ground, prices drop. Additionally, there's the issue that some gold deposits simply can't be mined or are much too expensive to extract.

While the company is building the mine, the price of shares will remain stable and will only start to rise once the date of effective production gets closer. Once the mine is up and running, other factors intervene in the price of shares, including the management's ability to increase production, reserves and cash flow.

The more you know about what stage of the life cycle the company is in, the better your chances are of minimizing risk and increasing your returns.

A Few Closing Words about Investing in Precious Metals

Undoubtedly, investing in precious metals is a wise course of action but before you do, you need to ensure you have a good grasp of the industry and the market as a whole to minimize risk.

You need to establish your objectives, namely why you want to invest in precious metals, and you can then design your investment plan accordingly.

Glossary of Gold and Silver Bullion Terms

Ask: the price at which a dealer offers to sell.

Assay: a test to ascertain the fineness and weight of a precious metal.

Bid: the price at which a dealer is willing to buy.

Boiler room: an enterprise that uses high pressure sales tactics, false or misleading information, and scare tactics, generally over the telephone, to sell overpriced or worthless investments to unsophisticated investors.

Bullion: precious metals in the form of bars that are at least 99.5% pure.

Bullion coin: a coin with a symbolic face value but trades at a price relative to its intrinsic value.

Call: the right, but not an obligation, to buy a commodity or a financial security on a specified date in the future.

Canadian Maple Leafs: modern bullion coins minted by the Royal Canadian Mint.

Chameleon: a broker or dealer who changes his position on an investment to what he thinks will cause an investor to enter into a transaction.

Comex: one of the world's major commodities futures exchanges where gold and silver are traded. The Comex is in New York City and is a division of the New York Mercantile Exchange.

Fiat money: paper money made legal tender by law, although not backed by gold or silver.

Gold standard: a monetary system based on convertibility into gold; paper money backed and interchangeable with gold.

Hallmark: mark or stamp on a bullion item that identifies the producer.

Intrinsic value: the value of a coin's metal content.

Kilo bar: a bar weighing one kilogram (32.1507 troy ounces).

Koala: Australian platinum coin, minted since 1987,.995 fine.

Krugerrand: South African gold coin.

Liquidity: the quality of being readily convertible into cash.

NYMEX: the New York Mercantile Exchange, a future exchange where platinum and palladium are traded.

PCGS: acronym for Professional Coin Grading Service, one of two major coin grading services in the United States.

Silver Eagles: modern 1-oz silver bullion coins.

Uncirculated: a coin in new condition, sometimes said to be "brilliant uncirculated" or "BU." The term is often used interchangeably with Mint State.

Suppliers of Investment Quality Gold and Silver Bullion Bars and Coins

ATS BULLION LTD
International Bullion Merchants

http://www.atsbullion.com

Weighton Coin Wonders

Specialists in Gold and Silver
Coins & Sets

http://www.weightoncoin.co.uk

Tax Free Gold Coins & Bars ⊠
www.taxfreegold.co.uk

American Precious Metals Exchange

APMEX is one of the largest and most
active precious metal dealers.

http://www.apmex.com

Chards is a leading UK coin and bullion dealer.
http://www.chards.co.uk

Gold and Silver Bullion Bars and Coins
Delivery is offered to all residents in the
UK and within the EU
http://www.bullionuk.com

The Perth Mint Australia
The Perth Mint, Western Australia,
manufactures and distributes platinum,
silver and gold coins.
http://www.perthmint.com.au

www.ingramcontent.com/pod-product-compliance
Lightning Source LLC
Chambersburg PA
CBHW071611170526
45166CB00003B/1059